THIS WALKER BOOK BELONGS TO:

....

....

....

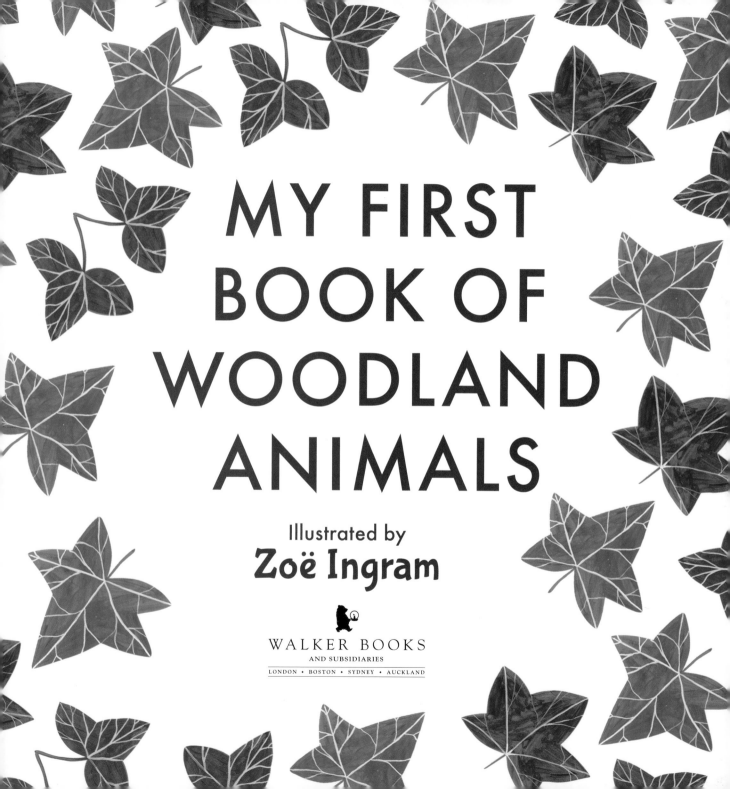

MY FIRST BOOK OF WOODLAND ANIMALS

Illustrated by
Zoë Ingram

WALKER BOOKS
AND SUBSIDIARIES
LONDON • BOSTON • SYDNEY • AUCKLAND

Fox

Known for its stealth and cunning, the red fox is a type of wild dog. Foxes have a large number of calls that they use to talk to each other. They also wag their tails to communicate – just like pet dogs. A female fox is called a vixen.

Tracks

2.5 cm wide
5 cm long

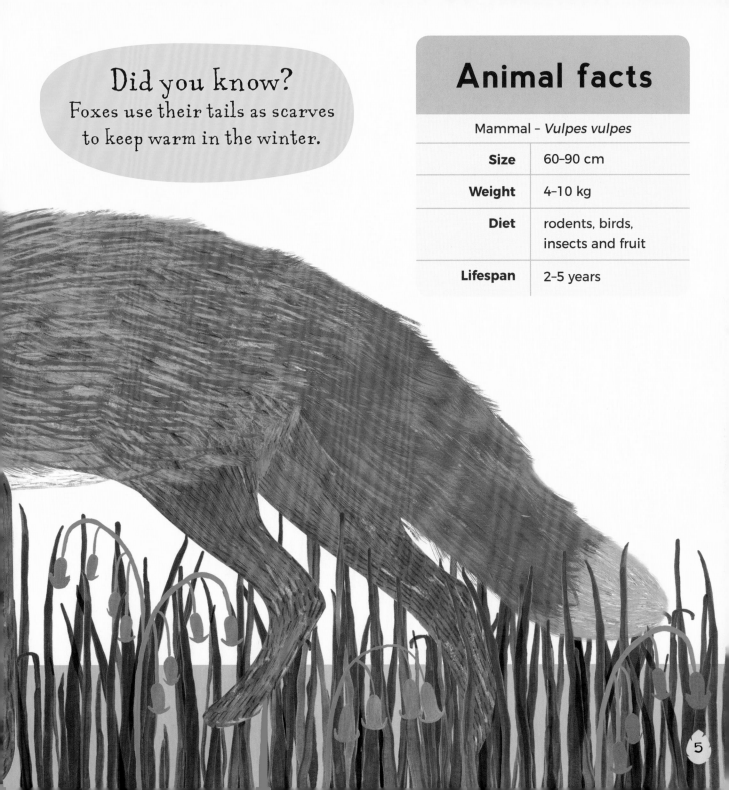

Did you know?
Foxes use their tails as scarves to keep warm in the winter.

Animal facts

Mammal - *Vulpes vulpes*

Size	60–90 cm
Weight	4–10 kg
Diet	rodents, birds, insects and fruit
Lifespan	2–5 years

Animal facts

Mammal – *Meles meles*	
Size	60–90 cm
Weight	10–12 kg
Diet	worms, but just about anything
Lifespan	up to 14 years

Did you know?
Some of the largest setts have up to 100 different rooms!

Badger

This unmistakable nocturnal animal lives in friendly family groups of five to ten badgers. They dig down into the ground to build their home, or sett. The male is called a boar and the female a sow. Baby badgers are called cubs.

Tracks

3.5 cm wide
4.5 cm long

Honey bee

Wild honey bees build their nests in hollow trees, protected from wind and rain. They are extremely sociable creatures and live in groups of up to 80,000 in the summer. Bees are vital to the food chain as they pollinate the crops that provide our food.

Larvae

Larvae hatch after 3 days and grow up to 1,500 times their size in just 5 days.

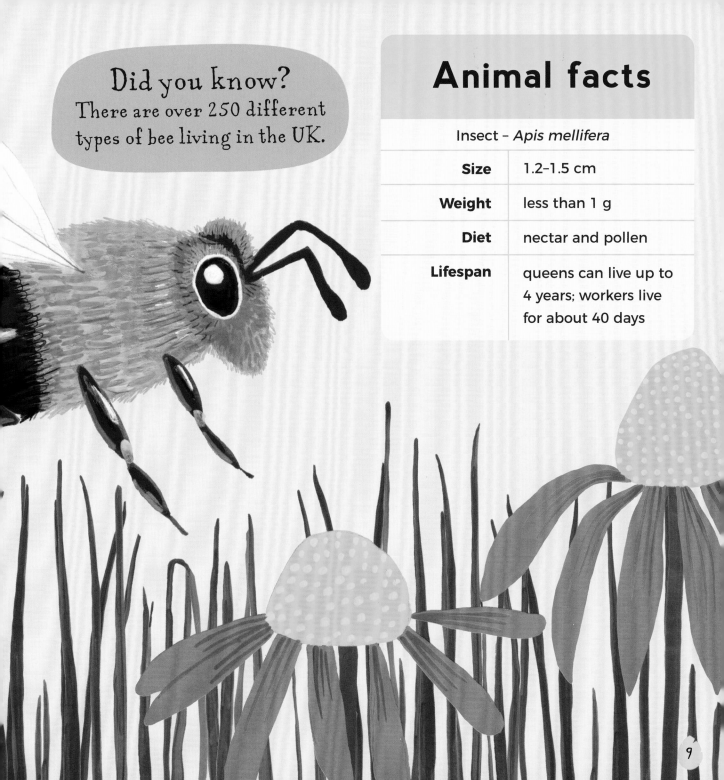

Did you know?
There are over 250 different types of bee living in the UK.

Animal facts

Insect – *Apis mellifera*

Size	1.2–1.5 cm
Weight	less than 1 g
Diet	nectar and pollen
Lifespan	queens can live up to 4 years; workers live for about 40 days

Animal facts

Mammal – *Oryctolagus cuniculus*	
Size	35–45 cm
Weight	1–2.5 kg
Diet	leaves, shoots, grass and bark
Lifespan	3 years

Rabbit

Rabbits are friendly animals and one of the UK's most common mammals. They build their large groups of burrows, known as warrens, in deciduous woodland. A single female rabbit, or doe, can have 100 babies in a year. Baby rabbits are known as kittens.

Tracks

Fore: 2.5 cm x 2.5 cm
Hind: 2.5 cm wide x 3.5 cm long

Frog

The common frog is an amphibian, which means it lives on land but lays its eggs in water. Frogs have smooth skin and long legs that are good for jumping. They lay their eggs (or spawn) in large clumps during springtime and when the eggs hatch, they are called tadpoles.

Larvae

Tadpoles hatch after 6–21 days and become froglets in 12–16 weeks.

Animal facts

Amphibian – *Rana temporaria*

Size	8–13 cm
Weight	22 g
Diet	worms, slugs, snails, insects and smaller amphibians
Lifespan	5–10 years

Did you know?
A female frog can lay up to 5,000 eggs in one year.

Animal facts

Mammal – *Mustela nivalis*	
Size	15–20 cm
Weight	60–115 g
Diet	voles, mice and small birds
Lifespan	2 years

Weasel

Weasels are the smallest of the UK's carnivores (meat-eaters) and very good hunters. They are small enough to get into a mouse's burrow and agile enough to climb trees and raid birds' nests. They have two or three litters of six kits every year and live in dens.

Tracks

2 cm wide

2.2 cm long

15

Bat

Pipistrelles are tiny bats. Bats are nocturnal – which means that they sleep during the day and come out at night. You are most likely to see them at dusk as they fly out of their nests to catch insects. They have incredible hearing.

Droppings

Bats' shiny black poo can be up to **8 cm** long.

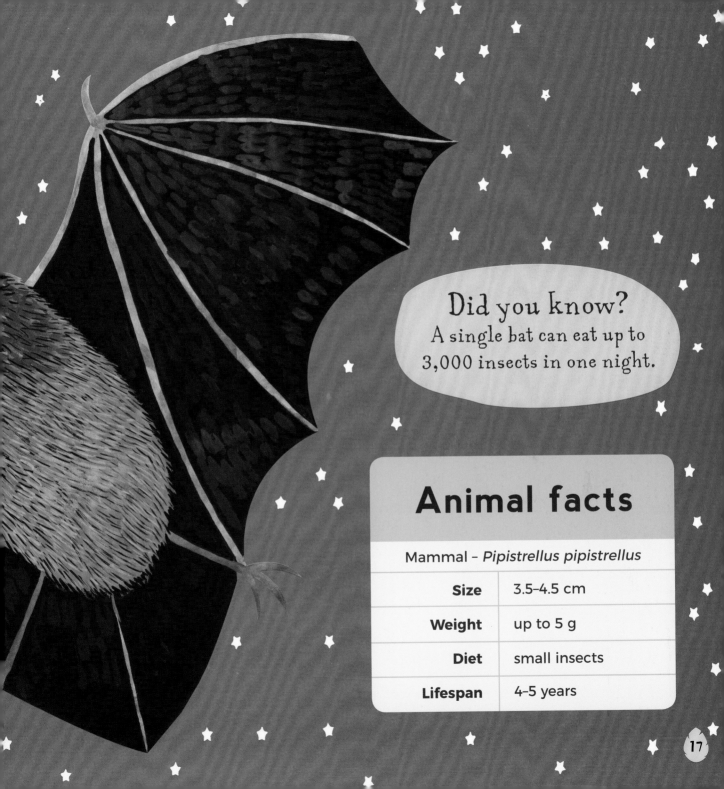

Did you know?
A single bat can eat up to 3,000 insects in one night.

Animal facts

Mammal – *Pipistrellus pipistrellus*

Size	3.5–4.5 cm
Weight	up to 5 g
Diet	small insects
Lifespan	4–5 years

Animal facts

Mammal – *Cervus elaphus*

Size	1.4 m at the shoulder
Weight	up to 200 kg
Diet	grass, herbs, roots, fungi, tree shoots
Lifespan	16–18 years

Did you know?
The pattern of a stag's antlers is as unique as your fingerprint.

Red deer

The red deer is the largest land mammal in the UK. An adult male deer (or stag) has antlers made out of bone, covered in a velvety skin. They use their antlers to show how strong they are and grow a brand new set every year. A female deer is called a doe.

Tracks

7 cm wide
9 cm long

Water vole

This protected species lives beside rivers and streams. They are great swimmers and trap bubbles of air in their fur to keep themselves warm in the water. Their burrows, which they build in riverbanks, have different levels so that they don't flood.

Did you know? Despite his name, Ratty from *The Wind in the Willows* is actually a water vole.

Tracks

Fore: 2 cm x 2 cm
Hind: 2.2 cm wide x 3.4 cm long

Animal facts

Mammal – *Arvicola amphibius*

Size	12–20 cm (tail 7–11 cm)
Weight	80–180 g
Diet	water plants and grasses
Lifespan	up to 3 years

Animal facts

Insect – *Lucanus cervus*	
Size	3.5–7.5 cm
Weight	Up to 25 g
Diet	the grubs eat decaying wood
Lifespan	6 years

Stag beetle

The stag beetle is the largest UK land beetle. They live right on the edge of woodland and spend most of their lives underground as larvae. The male's jaws are shaped like a deer's antlers, which is how they get their name.

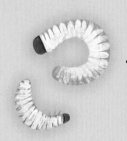

Larvae

The female lays up to 21 eggs, which grow into larvae up to 8 cm long.

Hedgehog

The hedgehog is a shy, nocturnal creature. They have poor eyesight and rely on their smell and hearing. When they are frightened (and when they hibernate) they curl up into a prickly protective ball. A group of hedgehogs is called an array and a baby hedgehog is called a hoglet.

Did you know?
An average hedgehog has over 5,000 prickles.

Tracks

2.8 cm wide
2.5 cm long

24

Animal facts

Mammal – *Erinaceus europaeus*

Size	22–30 cm
Weight	0.5–1.5 kg
Diet	worms, slugs, earwigs and eggs
Lifespan	2–5 years

Animal facts

Insect – *Polygonia c-album*

Size	5.5–6 cm
Weight	less than 1 g
Diet	nectar from wildflowers such as thistles
Lifespan	up to a year

Did you know?
The white commas (**,**) marked on the underside of their wings give them their name.

Comma butterfly

Comma butterflies can be seen all year round. In the last century their numbers in the UK dropped dramatically, but they have made an amazing comeback. Their speckled wings help them to blend in with their surroundings, avoiding predators.

Caterpillars

3.2–4 cm long

Mole

These instantly recognizable animals are very hard to spot as they spend almost all of their lives underground. They have short velvety fur and long curved claws for digging. They are almost blind but they have an incredible sense of smell.

Tracks

You are far more likely to see a molehill than mole tracks.

Animal facts

Mammal – *Talpa europaea*

Size	12–15 cm
Weight	60–130 g
Diet	earthworms, slugs and insect larvae
Lifespan	3–4 years

Did you know?
Moles can dig up to 20 metres of tunnel in a single day.

Animal facts

Mammal – *Lutra lutra*	
Size	55–90 cm
Weight	5–10 kg
Diet	fish, frogs, small birds and mammals
Lifespan	5–8 years

Did you know?
Fresh otter poo (spraint) smells like jasmine tea!

Otter

The otter is an internationally protected species that very nearly became extinct in the twentieth century because of pollution and habitat destruction. Otters have large territories and give birth to their cubs in underground burrows known as holts.

Tracks

6 cm wide
9 cm long

Goat moth

One of the largest UK moths, the goat moth lives in deciduous woodland. They lay their eggs on the bark of a tree and when they hatch, the large caterpillars burrow into the wood, where they live for up to five years. Like most moths, goat moths fly at night.

Caterpillars

Up to 10 cm long

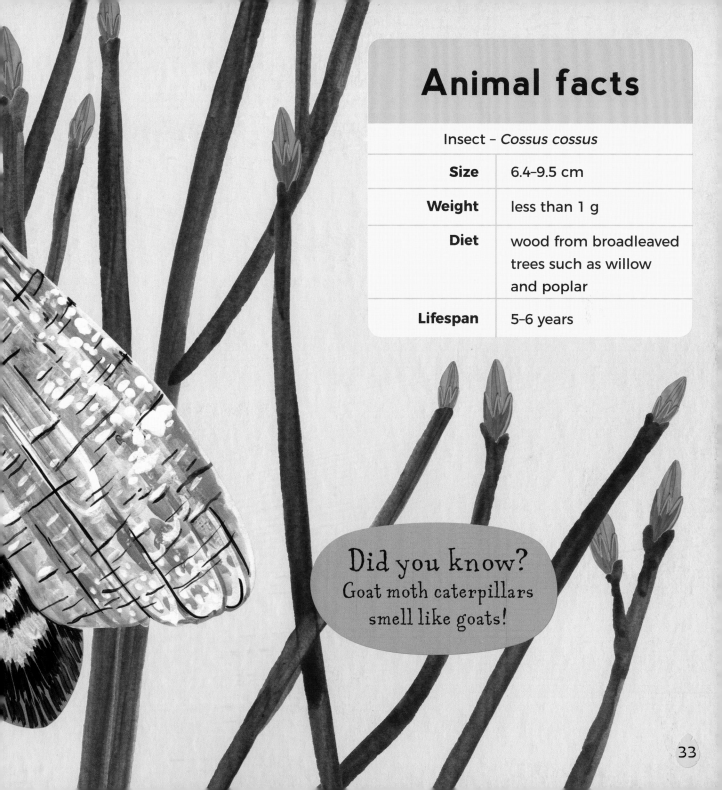

Animal facts

Insect – *Cossus cossus*	
Size	6.4–9.5 cm
Weight	less than 1 g
Diet	wood from broadleaved trees such as willow and poplar
Lifespan	5–6 years

Did you know?
Goat moth caterpillars
smell like goats!

Animal facts

Bird – *Strix aluco*	
Size	37–39 cm
Weight	330–590 g
Diet	rodents, small birds, frogs, fish, insects
Lifespan	5 years

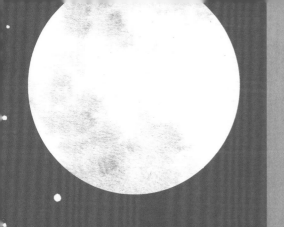

Tawny owl

Although this nocturnal bird is the most common owl in the UK, it can be hard to spot. Keep an eye out for pellets and poo on the woodland floor underneath their roosting sites. Tawny owls can turn their heads 270 degrees to look right behind themselves!

Did you know?
The familiar call of the tawny owl is actually made by two birds. The female owl calls "tuwit" and the male calls "tuwoo".

Eggs
Egg size: 4.8 x 3.9 cm
Clutch size: 2–3

Grey squirrel

Grey squirrels are one of the most familiar woodland animals. They are bigger, stronger and more adaptable than native red squirrels, outnumbering them by fifteen to one. They make their nest, called a drey, out of twigs. Squirrel babies are called kits.

Tracks

Fore: 2.5 cm wide x 3.5 cm long
Hind: 3.5 cm wide x 4.5 cm long

Did you know?
Squirrels often forget where they have buried their nuts in the autumn!

Animal facts

Mammal – *Sciurus carolinensis*	
Size	23–30 cm
Weight	450–650 g
Diet	acorns, bulbs, shoots, fungi, nuts, seeds
Lifespan	2–6 years

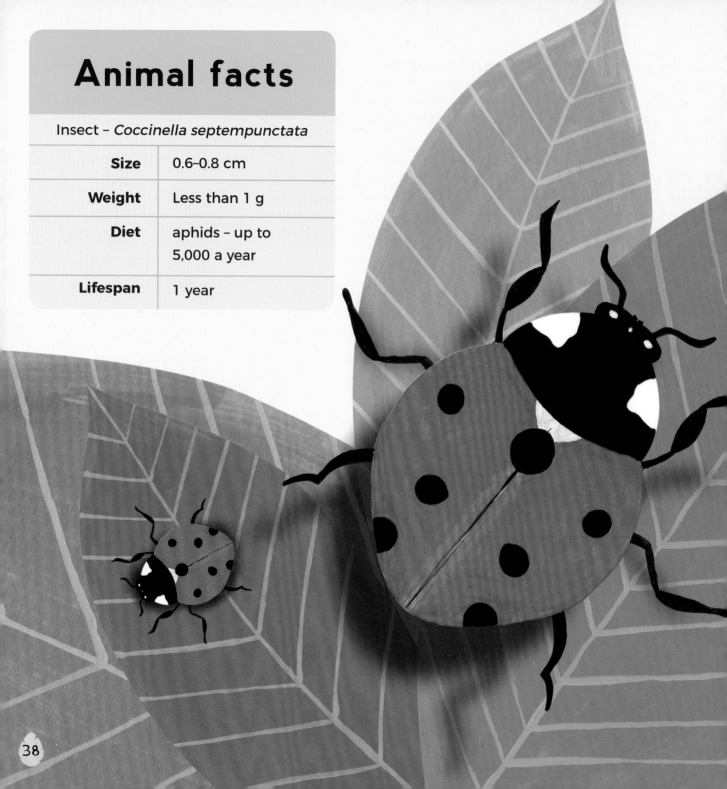

Animal facts

Insect – *Coccinella septempunctata*

Size	0.6–0.8 cm
Weight	Less than 1 g
Diet	aphids – up to 5,000 a year
Lifespan	1 year

Seven-spot ladybird

The most common of over 40 species of British ladybird, the seven-spotted type lays bright yellow eggs which then hatch into grubs. Ladybirds come in different bright colours to warn off predators.

Larvae
Up to 1.3 cm long

Did you know?
Ladybirds can fly at up to 60 km per hour.

Grass snake

This is the largest snake in the UK and is not venomous. The female is larger than the male and lays about 40 eggs in rotting vegetation. Like all reptiles, they hibernate through the winter months.

Eggs

Egg size: 2.3 x 3 cm
Clutch size: up to 40

Did you know?
Grass snakes are really good swimmers.

Animal facts

Reptile – *Natrix helvetica*	
Size	90–150 cm
Weight	up to 240 g
Diet	frogs, fish, birds, small mammals
Lifespan	15–25 years

Animal facts

Mammal – *Muscardinus avellanarius*	
Size	7–9 cm
Weight	15–40 g
Diet	nuts, seeds, flowers, fruit
Lifespan	5 years

Did you know?
Dormice are the only mice to have furry tails.

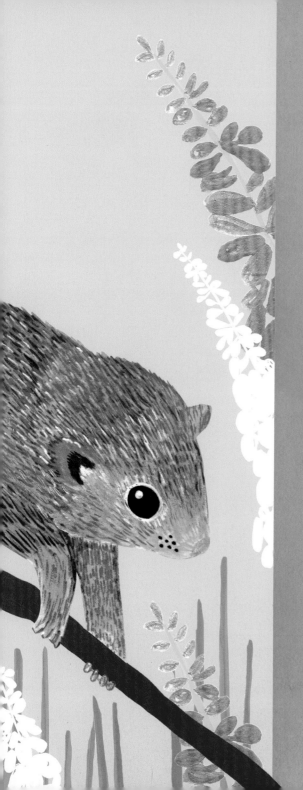

Dormouse

Also known as the hazel dormouse, this cute creature is protected in the UK. They are hard to spot as they are nocturnal and hibernate through the winter months in their cosy nests.

Tracks

If you see a hazelnut with a hole in, it was probably nibbled by a dormouse!

Index

Tick off the animals that you have seen in woodland or out and about.

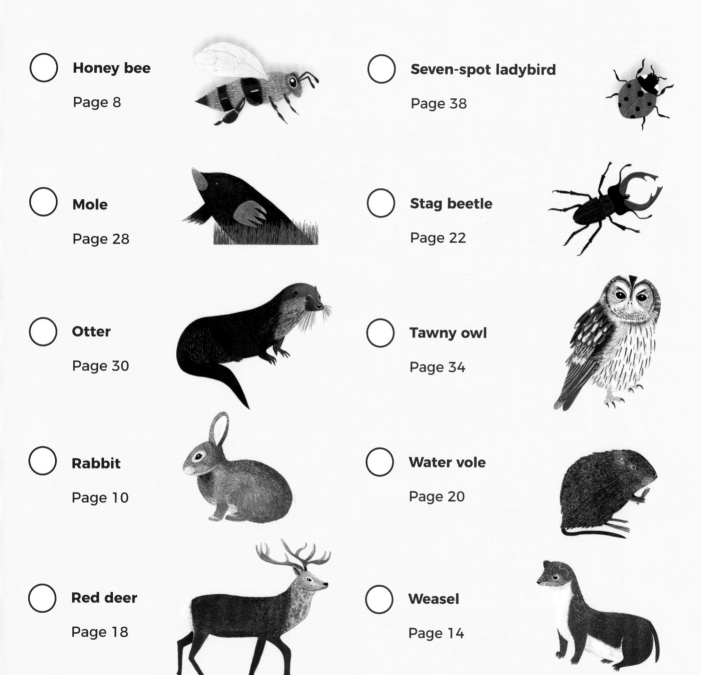

**For my little hedgehog and otter
who both love "skrirrels".
And Charlie.**

First published 2020 by Walker Books Ltd
87 Vauxhall Walk, London SE11 5HJ

This edition published 2021 for Scottish Book Trust
Scottish charity, SC027669

2 4 6 8 10 9 7 5 3 1

This book has been typeset in Futura, Montserrat,
Nevis and Aunt Mildred

Printed in China

British Library Cataloguing in Publication Data:
a catalogue record for this book is available
from the British Library

ISBN 978-1-5295-0368-5

www.walker.co.uk

FSC
www.fsc.org

MIX
Paper from
responsible sources
FSC® C104723